The Impact of NLP Techniques on Conflict Resolution and Negotiation Skills

By Rex Morton

Copyright Page

information the organization or website may provide or recommendations it might make. Furthermore, the author does not guarantee the accuracy of the information these resources provide.

The use of any information provided in this book is solely at your own risk.

Chapter 1: Introduction

Before we delve into the intertwining complexities of Neuro-Linguistic Programming (NLP), conflict resolution, and negotiation skills, it's vital to establish a common understanding of these terms.

A. Definition of Key Terms

Neuro-Linguistic Programming (NLP): This psychological strategy entails studying the tactics employed by successful people and using them to further a personal objective. It links ideas, words, and behavioural patterns acquired via experience to certain results. NLP, which was developed in the 1970s by Richard Bandler and John Grinder, frequently uses hypnosis and self-hypnosis to help people make the necessary changes.

Conflict Resolution: This is a means for two or more parties to settle their dispute in a peaceful manner. The disagreement may be personal, financial, political, or emotional. When a dispute arises, often the best course of action is negotiation to resolve the disagreement. In the process, conflict resolution aims to promote constructive communication, understanding, and collaboration between the conflicting parties.

Negotiation Skills: These are qualities that allow two or more parties to reach a mutual agreement. They are critical in sales and business environments to drive agreement between different parties with varying views and interests. Good negotiation skills involve excellent communication, understanding of human psychology, strategic planning, and the ability to influence outcomes favorably.

B. Overview of the Relationship Between NLP, Conflict Resolution, and Negotiation Skills

NLP, conflict resolution, and negotiation skills intertwine in various ways. At the heart of conflict resolution and negotiation lie effective communication and understanding—core principles that NLP is designed to enhance. By understanding and harnessing the power of language and thought patterns, individuals can better manage their responses to conflicts and negotiate more effectively.

NLP offers practical tools and techniques that can improve communication, build rapport, create mutual understanding, and influence behavior—essential elements in both conflict resolution and negotiation. While the latter two often present in formal, high-stakes environments, such as diplomatic negotiations or business deals, they are equally applicable to everyday interactions and disputes.

C. Purpose and Structure of the Book

This book aims to explore in detail how NLP techniques can profoundly impact conflict resolution and negotiation skills. It provides a comprehensive analysis, from theoretical foundations to practical applications, including relevant case studies.

Following this introduction, we will delve into separate chapters exploring NLP, conflict resolution, and negotiation skills in detail. Subsequent chapters will examine the intersections of these areas and how NLP can be practically applied to enhance conflict resolution and negotiation skills. We will also discuss controversies surrounding NLP and ponder its future, particularly in conflict resolution and negotiation.

Whether you're a student of psychology, a professional negotiator, or someone interested in improving your interpersonal skills, this book offers insightful knowledge and practical tools. By the end, you will understand the transformative power of NLP and how it can be utilized to resolve conflicts more effectively and negotiate with enhanced skill and confidence.

A. History and Evolution of NLP

Neuro-Linguistic Programming was born in the 1970s out of a collaboration between Richard Bandler, a computer scientist and Gestalt therapist, and John Grinder, a linguist. The duo observed leading therapists in their field, including Virginia Satir, Milton Erickson, and Fritz Perls, and replicated their successful strategies, thus giving birth to NLP.

Over the years, NLP has evolved into a toolkit for personal development and communication. It's been used across diverse fields, from business coaching to sports performance and from education to therapy. Despite ongoing debates about its scientific validity, it's attracted a wide user base due to its focus on practical results.

B. Core Principles of NLP

NLP rests on several core principles:

The Map is not the Territory: This principle highlights the distinction between our perception of reality and reality itself. Everyone has a unique "map" of the world, shaped by individual experiences and beliefs.

Experience has a Structure: Our thoughts and behaviors follow patterns, and by understanding and modifying these patterns, we can change our responses and outcomes.

If One Person Can Do Something, Anyone Can Learn to Do It: NLP holds that skills and abilities aren't exclusive traits but can be modeled and replicated using the right approach.

Mind and Body are Parts of the Same System: Our thoughts and emotions influence our physical state and vice versa.

We Always Have a Choice: Believing in multiple possible responses to any situation, NLP encourages flexibility and adaptability in thinking and behavior.

C. Common NLP Techniques

NLP offers an array of techniques, including:

Anchoring: This involves associating a physical stimulus with a psychological state. Like a particular song evoking specific emotions, an "anchor" can trigger desired responses.

Reframing: This technique changes the context or meaning of a perceived problem or situation, thereby altering its emotional impact.

Swish Pattern: This NLP technique is about replacing an undesirable state or reaction with a desirable one.

Visual/Kinesthetic Dissociation (V/KD): This technique helps individuals distance themselves from distressing experiences or memories, reducing their emotional impact.

D. Hypothetical Case Studies of NLP Application in Different Fields

Education: A teacher struggling with an unruly class uses NLP to build rapport. By observing and mirroring students' body language and speech patterns, she establishes a connection with them. Coupling this with anchoring positive behavior, the classroom dynamic transforms significantly.

Business: A sales team adopts NLP techniques to enhance their communication with customers. They employ reframing to present their products positively and overcome objections. Additionally, the use of V/KD helps them deal with rejection and maintain a positive mindset.

Therapy: A therapist uses the Swish Pattern technique with a client suffering from anxiety. The client learns to replace anxious thoughts with empowering ones, leading to a significant decrease in anxiety levels.

Sports: A coach uses NLP to boost a team's morale. He uses anchoring to associate feelings of confidence and unity with a particular team chant. This leads to improved performance and increased team cohesion during matches.

As we can see, NLP, despite controversies, provides practical tools that can be instrumental in various areas of life. It's in the arenas of conflict resolution and negotiation, however, where NLP truly shines—a subject we'll explore in upcoming chapters.

A. Understanding the Nature of Conflict

Conflict arises when there is a perceived threat to our needs, interests, or concerns. It is an integral part of human interaction, and while often seen as negative, it can also lead to growth and innovation. Conflicts can occur at the individual, group, or organizational level and can be interpersonal, intrapersonal, intergroup, or intragroup.

Understanding the nature of conflict involves recognizing its source (competing needs, interests, or goals), its levels (latent, perceived, felt, manifest, aftermath), and its types (constructive or destructive).

B. Conflict Resolution Theories and Models

Several theories and models guide conflict resolution:

Thomas-Kilmann Conflict Mode Instrument (TKI): It identifies five conflict-handling styles based on levels of assertiveness and cooperativeness—avoidance, accommodation, competition, compromise, and collaboration.

Interest-Based Relational (IBR) Approach: This approach focuses on protecting relationships by separating people from the problem and prioritizing mutual interests over individual positions.

Transactional Analysis (TA): Eric Berne's theory focuses on interactions ("transactions") between people, recognizing three ego states—Parent, Adult, and Child. Effective conflict resolution tends to occur in Adult-Adult transactions.

C. Role of Effective Communication in Conflict Resolution

Effective communication is critical in conflict resolution. It promotes understanding, reduces hostility, and can turn a potentially negative situation into a positive one. Key components include active listening (fully focusing, understanding, responding, and then remembering what is being said), emotional intelligence (understanding and managing your emotions to communicate effectively, empathize with others, overcome challenges, and defuse conflict), nonverbal cues, and assertiveness.

D. Hypothetical Case Studies on Successful Conflict Resolution

Workplace Conflict: Two colleagues, Alice and Bob, are in conflict over the distribution of tasks. Instead of resorting to office politics, they choose to engage in a facilitated conflict resolution process. By openly communicating their interests, they realize the unfair distribution of tasks and collaboratively decide on a more balanced workload.

Community Dispute: A community dispute arises over the proposed construction of a commercial complex in a residential area. The local council organizes a town meeting, employing an IBR approach. By separating the conflicting parties from the problem and focusing on shared interests, they come to a resolution—small-scale, eco-friendly businesses that benefit the community.

International Diplomacy: Country A and B are in a territorial dispute. They enter into diplomatic negotiations, where both countries communicate their interests clearly. They agree to resolve their differences through the international court instead of escalating military tension.

Family Conflict: Two siblings, Sarah and John, are in conflict over their late father's will. They opt to seek the help of a mediator. Through clear communication and understanding of each other's interests and emotional attachment, they agree to an equitable distribution, preserving their relationship.

These hypothetical cases demonstrate the power of effective conflict resolution in diverse situations. In the following chapters, we will explore how NLP techniques can enrich this process further, providing unique tools to enhance negotiation and conflict resolution skills.

A. Understanding Negotiation: Definition and Types

Negotiation refers to a process where two or more parties with differing interests come together to find a common ground and reach an agreement. It is an essential aspect of human interaction, ranging from business deals and diplomatic treaties to personal situations.

There are several types of negotiation:

Distributive Negotiation: Also known as "win-lose" or "zero-sum" negotiation, it occurs when the parties are competing over limited resources.

Integrative Negotiation: Known as "win-win" negotiation, it involves collaboration between parties to find a mutually beneficial solution.

Multi-party Negotiation: This involves more than two parties and is usually more complex due to the number of interests and dynamics involved.

B. Essential Negotiation Strategies and Techniques

Several strategies and techniques can enhance negotiation outcomes:

Preparation and Planning: Understanding one's needs and interests, as well as those of the other party, is crucial. Research and proper planning can provide an upper hand in negotiations.

Active Listening: Listening attentively to the other party allows for better understanding and response.

Building Rapport: Establishing a positive connection can lead to more collaborative negotiations.

BATNA (Best Alternative to a Negotiated Agreement): Knowing your BATNA provides a negotiator with leverage and helps in making informed decisions.

C. Role of Emotional Intelligence in Negotiation

Negotiation requires a high level of emotional intelligence. It allows one to recognize and understand their emotions and the emotions of others, enabling effective management of emotions during the negotiation process. High emotional intelligence leads to better relationship management, empathetic listening, and ultimately more successful negotiations.

D. Hypothetical Case Studies Showcasing Effective Negotiation

Business Negotiation: A software company, Alpha, and a client negotiate the terms of a contract. By understanding their respective interests and needs through thorough preparation and active listening, they engage in an integrative negotiation process. Both parties leave the negotiation satisfied, establishing a long-term business relationship.

Diplomatic Negotiation: Two countries are in talks to establish a trade agreement. Through effective use of emotional intelligence, the negotiators manage their emotions and understand the emotions of the opposing side, leading to a successful negotiation of a mutually beneficial trade agreement.

Salary Negotiation: John, a job candidate, is negotiating his salary with a potential employer. He has a clear understanding of his BATNA and manages to negotiate a salary package that aligns with his skills and experience.

Real Estate Negotiation: A couple is negotiating the price of a house with a seller. By building rapport with the seller and effectively communicating their interest, they negotiate a reduction in the house price.

Through these hypothetical cases, the importance of negotiation skills in various fields becomes apparent. In the next chapters, we'll examine how these skills can be significantly enhanced by the strategic application of NLP techniques.

Chapter 5: The Intersection of NLP, Conflict Resolution, and Negotiation

A. Exploring the Link Between NLP and Conflict Resolution

NLP and conflict resolution are deeply interconnected. NLP's focus on understanding and altering thought patterns and behaviors aligns with the need to understand conflicts and devise effective strategies to resolve them.

For instance, the NLP technique of reframing can be a powerful tool in conflict resolution. It helps individuals view the conflict from different perspectives, fostering empathy and understanding. Anchoring, another NLP technique, can help individuals establish positive emotional states during the resolution process, facilitating constructive dialogue.

Moreover, NLP's emphasis on effective communication and understanding others' "world maps" enables individuals to appreciate different perspectives during conflicts, aiding in the resolution process.

B. How NLP Influences Negotiation Processes

The negotiation process can be considerably influenced by NLP. Negotiators can better control their responses to negotiations by comprehending and using the power of language and cognitive patterns.

NLP techniques such as rapport building can create a conducive environment for negotiation, enhancing trust and openness. Similarly, the use of reframing can help negotiators present their points more persuasively and handle objections better.

Further, NLP principles, such as 'the map is not the territory,' remind negotiators that their perspective is not the only one, encouraging them to understand and appreciate the opposing party's interests and concerns.

C. Review of Empirical Studies on the Intersection of NLP, Conflict Resolution, and Negotiation

Though empirical research on the intersection of NLP, conflict resolution, and negotiation is still evolving, some studies highlight the potential benefits:

Study on NLP and Conflict Resolution: A study by Michael Grinder explored the application of NLP in managing classroom conflicts. The study found that teachers using NLP techniques experienced improved classroom dynamics and reduced conflicts.

Research on NLP in Negotiation: In a research paper by Philip G. Clampitt, NLP techniques were employed in business negotiations, demonstrating an increased rate of successful outcomes. The study concluded that understanding and using verbal and non-verbal cues (key elements of NLP) can significantly enhance negotiation results.

Investigation into NLP, Mediation, and Negotiation: A study by John Burton explored the use of NLP techniques in mediation and negotiation. The research suggested that NLP could help mediators and negotiators enhance their communication skills and their ability to understand others, leading to more effective resolutions.

In the following chapters, we'll delve into practical applications and examples of how NLP techniques can be harnessed to improve conflict resolution and negotiation outcomes.

A. NLP Techniques for Managing Conflict Situations

Reframing: Helps to view the conflict from different perspectives, fostering empathy and understanding among conflicting parties. For example, a perceived negative criticism could be reframed as constructive feedback aimed at personal growth.

Anchoring: Enables individuals to manage their emotional states during conflict, maintaining a calm and constructive disposition. For instance, a person could anchor a state of calmness to a physical action such as deep breathing, activating it during a conflict situation.

Rapport Building: Fosters trust and openness, facilitating better communication. It could involve mirroring body language or matching the tone and pace of speech of the other person.

Visual/Kinesthetic Dissociation (V/KD): Helps individuals distance themselves from the immediate emotional intensity of a conflict, enabling them to think clearly and respond effectively.

**B. Hypothetical Case Studies Demonstrating the Use of NLP in
Resolving Conflicts**

Workplace Conflict: Emma and Jack, two colleagues, have a
conflict due to a misunderstanding about a project's deadlines.
Emma decides to use NLP techniques for conflict resolution. She
uses rapport building to foster a non-confrontational dialogue.
She applies anchoring to maintain a calm demeanor during their
discussion. Emma also uses reframing to present her
perspective, turning the conflict into a learning opportunity for
better communication. This approach helps to resolve the
conflict and improves their working relationship.

Family Dispute: A long-standing family dispute over a property
inheritance has caused significant strain within the family. One
of the family members, Lily, has been studying NLP and decides
to apply it to resolve this conflict. Lily initiates a family meeting
and employs V/KD to manage the emotionally charged
environment. She uses reframing to help everyone see the
dispute from different perspectives, encouraging empathy and
understanding. With the help of these techniques, the family
manages to resolve the dispute amicably.

C. Evaluation of Effectiveness: Pros and Cons

Pros:

Empathy and Understanding: NLP techniques like reframing promote empathy and understanding, key ingredients in conflict resolution.

Better Communication: Techniques like rapport building facilitate open and honest communication, helping to address the root causes of conflict.

Emotional Management: Techniques like anchoring and V/KD allow individuals to manage their emotional responses during conflict, promoting a more productive resolution process.

Cons:

Misuse: NLP techniques, if used manipulatively, can potentially harm relationships and exacerbate conflicts.

Training Required: To effectively use NLP in conflict resolution, a certain level of knowledge and skill is required. It may not be easily accessible or understandable to everyone.

Limitations in Severe Conflicts: While NLP can be beneficial in many conflict situations, it may have limited effectiveness in severe conflicts or disputes where legal or professional intervention is necessary.

The use of NLP techniques in conflict resolution offers exciting possibilities. However, it's crucial to use these tools ethically and consider professional help when conflicts escalate beyond manageable levels. In the next chapter, we'll examine how NLP can enhance negotiation skills and improve negotiation outcomes.

A. NLP Techniques That Enhance Negotiation Skills

Reframing: Reframing can be used in negotiation to reshape perceptions and persuade the other party. For instance, a price point could be reframed from "costly" to "investment," changing the perceived value.

Anchoring: Anchoring can help a negotiator maintain a state of confidence or calm during high-stakes negotiations. For example, a negotiator could use a visual anchor, such as an image of a successful past negotiation, to keep themselves focused and calm.

Rapport Building: Building rapport can foster trust and openness in negotiations, making the other party more receptive. Mirroring language, body language, and vocal tonality can create a subconscious connection and facilitate smoother negotiations.

Pacing and Leading: This technique involves matching the other party's behavior or emotional state (pacing) and then gradually changing your behavior to lead them towards a desired state or action.

**B. Hypothetical Case Studies Demonstrating the Use of NLP in
Negotiation**

Business Negotiation: In a negotiation between a software
company, Gamma, and a client, the Gamma representative uses
NLP techniques. He uses rapport building to establish a
connection with the client. He then uses reframing to turn the
perception of high prices into an investment in quality. Finally,
he uses anchoring to maintain a confident demeanor
throughout the negotiation. This approach leads to a successful
agreement satisfying both parties.

Real Estate Negotiation: A real estate agent, Clara, is
negotiating the sale of a property. She uses pacing and leading
to build rapport and guide the potential buyers towards a
purchase. She mirrors the buyers' excitement about the
property (pacing), then subtly shifts her language to discuss
ownership and investment potential (leading). Coupled with
reframing the property's drawbacks as unique features, Clara
successfully closes the sale.

C. Evaluation of Effectiveness: Pros and Cons

Pros:

Enhanced Persuasion: Techniques like reframing and pacing and
leading can significantly enhance a negotiator's persuasive
abilities.

Improved Communication: Rapport building and anchoring can lead to more open, honest, and controlled communication, enhancing negotiation outcomes.

Emotional Control: Techniques like anchoring allow a negotiator to maintain a desired emotional state during negotiations, reducing the risk of impulsive or emotional decisions.

Cons:

Misuse: Like in conflict resolution, NLP techniques can be misused in negotiation for manipulative purposes.

Skill Requirement: Effective application of NLP techniques requires understanding and practice. Not everyone might have the time or resources to acquire these skills.

Not a Silver Bullet: While NLP can enhance negotiation skills, it may not always guarantee successful outcomes. Factors such as the negotiation environment, the other party's disposition, and the subject of negotiation also play significant roles.

In conclusion, the use of NLP techniques in negotiation can provide a significant advantage when used ethically and skillfully. In the following chapter, we will discuss real-world examples, case studies, and research findings that highlight the practical benefits and limitations of using NLP techniques in conflict resolution and negotiation.

A. Critiques of NLP

Despite its wide usage and potential benefits, NLP has faced numerous criticisms:

Lack of Empirical Support: Many critics point out that NLP's effectiveness lacks solid empirical evidence. While there are anecdotal accounts and qualitative studies demonstrating its benefits, comprehensive, controlled, and replicated studies are comparatively scarce.

Vague Definitions and Lack of Standardization: Critics have noted that NLP's foundational concepts, such as 'modeling' and 'representational systems,' are often poorly defined and inconsistently applied. This lack of standardization makes NLP difficult to test scientifically.

Overemphasis on Language: Some argue that NLP places too much emphasis on language and not enough on other factors influencing behavior, such as societal context, cultural norms, and biological factors.

B. Current Challenges in the Field

Misrepresentation and Misuse: Given its powerful influence on behavior, NLP can be misused for manipulative purposes. Additionally, some practitioners misrepresent NLP as a "quick fix" for complex psychological issues, leading to skepticism and misperceptions about the field.

Training and Qualification Standards: There's a lack of standardized training and qualification criteria for NLP practitioners, leading to concerns about the quality of practice.

Integration with Other Therapies: NLP faces challenges in integrating with other psychological therapies and counseling methods. It is often viewed as a stand-alone approach, limiting its interdisciplinary applications.

C. Addressing the Controversies and the Way Forward

Enhancing Empirical Research: To address criticisms regarding lack of empirical support, more rigorous, controlled, and replicated studies should be conducted to evaluate NLP's effectiveness in various applications, including conflict resolution and negotiation.

Standardization: Developing clear definitions, standardized practices, and qualification standards could help address concerns regarding NLP's scientific validity and the quality of NLP practice.

Ethical Practice and Regulation: Establishing ethical guidelines and regulatory standards can prevent misuse and misrepresentation of NLP. This includes promoting responsible and ethical use of NLP in conflict resolution and negotiation.

Collaboration and Integration: Encouraging interdisciplinary collaboration can help integrate NLP with other therapeutic and psychological approaches, enhancing its effectiveness and acceptance.

Despite the criticisms and challenges, NLP's potential in enhancing conflict resolution and negotiation skills cannot be ignored. By addressing these concerns, the field can move forward in a more rigorous, ethical, and integrative manner. In the next chapter, we'll discuss future directions for research and practice in this exciting and evolving field.

Chapter 9: The Future of NLP in Conflict Resolution and Negotiation

A. The Potential of Integrating NLP with Emerging Technologies

Artificial Intelligence and Machine Learning: AI and ML could be used to create sophisticated NLP-based applications and tools that aid in conflict resolution and negotiation. For instance, AI could analyze negotiation patterns and suggest NLP-based strategies in real-time.

Virtual Reality (VR): VR could be utilized to create immersive training environments where individuals can practice NLP techniques in simulated conflict or negotiation scenarios, allowing them to apply skills in a safe, controlled setting.

Natural Language Processing (the other NLP): This field of computer science, which shares an acronym with Neuro-Linguistic Programming, could be integrated to develop smart systems capable of detecting and interpreting language patterns, potentially enhancing the application of NLP techniques in virtual communication environments.

B. Trends and Future Research Directions

Empirical Studies: As discussed in previous chapters, there is a growing need for empirical studies that demonstrate the efficacy of NLP in conflict resolution and negotiation. Future research may focus on designing rigorous and replicable studies in this area.

NLP and Neuroscience: Future trends may involve further exploration of the neurological underpinnings of NLP techniques to provide a more scientific understanding of their impact on human behavior.

Cultural Relevance: Research could also focus on the cultural relevance and adaptability of NLP techniques, as effective conflict resolution and negotiation often require understanding and respect for cultural differences.

C. Potential Impact on Various Sectors – Business, Politics, Social Services, etc.

Business: In the corporate world, NLP could enhance communication, negotiation with clients and stakeholders, and resolution of internal conflicts, ultimately leading to increased productivity and a healthier work environment.

Politics: Politicians and diplomats could use NLP techniques to better negotiate policy, resolve disputes, and connect with their constituents, contributing to more effective governance.

Social Services: In sectors such as healthcare, education, and counseling, NLP could be used to manage conflicts and negotiate solutions effectively, leading to improved service delivery.

The future of NLP in conflict resolution and negotiation is full of possibilities. As we refine our understanding and enhance our practice, we can look forward to a world where conflicts are managed more effectively, and negotiations lead to more satisfying and beneficial outcomes for all parties involved. In the final chapter, we will recap the key points and consider some closing thoughts.

A. Summarization of Key Points

Neuro-Linguistic Programming (NLP): We delved into the principles, techniques, and history of NLP, understanding how it aims to model and change human behavior.

Conflict Resolution: We explored the theories, models, and the vital role of effective communication in managing and resolving conflicts.

Negotiation Skills: We discussed essential negotiation strategies and techniques, underlining the importance of emotional intelligence in successful negotiation.

Intersection of NLP, Conflict Resolution, and Negotiation: We explored how NLP techniques can enhance conflict resolution and negotiation processes and discussed empirical studies supporting this intersection.

Practical Applications: We highlighted specific NLP techniques that can be applied in conflict resolution and negotiation and discussed their effectiveness through hypothetical case studies.

Challenges and Controversies: We addressed the critiques of NLP and the challenges it faces, discussing potential solutions and the way forward.

Future of NLP in Conflict Resolution and Negotiation: We looked at potential integrations with emerging technologies, future research directions, and potential impacts on various sectors.

B. Practical Implications for Individuals and Organizations

For Individuals: NLP techniques can empower individuals with effective tools for managing personal and professional conflicts, and for negotiating successful outcomes in various areas of life.

For Organizations: Businesses, governments, and social service sectors can utilize NLP to foster a culture of effective communication, better conflict management, and enhanced negotiation skills, leading to improved decision-making, productivity, and service delivery.

C. Final Thoughts on the Future of NLP in Conflict Resolution and Negotiation

Despite its challenges and controversies, NLP holds immense potential in the realms of conflict resolution and negotiation. As we continue to explore its applications and validate its effectiveness through rigorous research, we can expect to see an increased adoption of NLP techniques in personal lives, professional environments, and broader societal contexts.

The path forward lies in responsible and ethical use of NLP, standardization of practices, and integration with emerging technologies and other therapeutic modalities. By embracing these principles, we can harness the full potential of NLP in transforming the landscape of conflict resolution and negotiation, thereby fostering a more cooperative, understanding, and productive society.

About the Author

Rex Morton is a renowned author and researcher in the United Kingdom with a passionate interest in the human mind, specifically in Cognitive Behavioural Therapy (CBT) and Neuro-Linguistic Programming (NLP).

Morton has spent a considerable portion of his professional life diving deep into the theories and principles that form the backbone of these two compelling fields. His fascination with NLP led him to complete an extensive certification program, solidifying his understanding of this innovative approach to understanding human behaviour.

Although Morton does not have clinical experience, his intense curiosity and dedication to studying these subjects have made him a respected figure in the field. He has thoroughly researched the integration of NLP techniques into CBT, offering fresh perspectives and insights into how these two methodologies can complement each other to enhance understanding of human cognition and behaviour.

As an author, Morton has successfully communicated his knowledge and passion to a broader audience, making complex psychological theories accessible to professionals and interested laypersons. His writing is characterized by a clear, engaging style and a focus on the practical application of theories, making them relevant to everyday life.

In his personal life, Morton is an ardent lover of the natural world, often spending his free time exploring the British countryside. His passion for landscape photography allows him to capture and share the beauty of these excursions. Despite his accomplishments, Morton is known for his humility and eagerness to continue learning. His work continues to inspire those interested in the intricate workings of the human mind and the exciting possibilities presented by the integration of NLP and CBT.

If you've found the content of this book enlightening and wish to continue your journey of understanding the human mind, I warmly invite you to visit my website at www.rexmorton.com. The website serves as a hub of knowledge where I share my latest findings, thoughts, and insights on the integration of NLP and CBT.

I also encourage you to subscribe to the newsletter available on the website. By subscribing, you'll receive regular updates on a range of topics, from detailed discussions on specific NLP techniques and their application in CBT, to the latest research in the field.

The newsletter is also the first place I'll share news of upcoming releases. Whether it's the announcement of a new book, the launch of an online course, newsletter subscribers will be the first to know. This is a great opportunity to continue learning directly from me, deepening your understanding of NLP and CBT, and enhancing your skills in applying these techniques in your own life or professional practice.

I'm looking forward to sharing this journey with you.